Tuberculosis
Blindr

"There will always be suffering. But we must not suffer over the suffering."
-Alan Watts

What do we do with a drunken sailor?

There sitting in the kitchen
Down the sides of the glass,
Watching the last drops glisten,
While In moments the hours passed.
Each spent quietly sipping.
Before journeying
From floor,
Back to his chair
Strangling the smooth neck of his lover,
Pulling her dark wavy hair.
Together wounded in a salted pool,
They had laid there.
Shattering glass to christen!
Reminiscent
When their lips first met
Their lifelong companionship.
Now sunken and missing.
No patrol will come,
No lifeboats set sail.
Whether it be at the bottom of the sea,
Or deep in the belly of a whale.
A ship Captained drunk will not
Fare-well.

"You're not depressed"
"It's just a passing feeling"
"Stop lying in bed"
"You'll go blind staring at the ceiling."
"Go outside you need fresh air."
"When was the last time you showered?"
"And go cut that greasy hair!"
"Why can't you smile?"
Are you physically impaired?

No.

I just realized
How little,
You care.

Is there a kingdom beyond this shore?
Some distant adventure?
To be restored.
Will my name be enshrined?
Across the annals,
Engraved upon slabs of stone?
Will people wish to see what I stood for?
Or shall I fade and drift
Like fallen ocean waves
My steps soaked
Erased by break of day
Tell me now
I would like to expose
Have you ever wondered
where it is,
You're meant to go?
Or am I simply dancing
Through A choreographed,
One man show.

The crest of the mountain
The breath of a fountain
Embraced through evergreen and
A softhearted plea
Mounting an expedition to needs
While I bleed and bleed
Beckoned by shouting
Running wishful, over piles,
Of dead, Molting leaves
Searching for a transparent eye
Casting its gaze
Current-less
Under a shimmering shawl
I saw in the cave
There!
Behind the waterfall
Beneath
The crest of the mountain
Shrouded in silver fountains
The genesis of roots
Wrapping my spirit
Within me,
Sprouting a seed
To return the breath that leaves
With hearty decree
Tis not all
what we are or seem.
Trapped wanders in a stunted dream
Find me walking
Beyond the crest of the mountain
Beneath the forever green

Come up from down there!
Can you feel it?
That choking despair!
You're looking left
To what's right-
Where?
The music lingering in the air?
What you cast off-
Those binding fears!
Flesh ripe to ensnare
Pull apart-
The entombed snare!
Until there.

Empty words.
Empty stares.

Come up from down there!
Rest for a moment
Leave behind their-
Shanked prayers!
Take my arm!
Let us relish in,
Ceremonious despair!
Lick our wounds
and carefully tend,
The burdens we bare.
Witness fire in the sky
Ice in our veins
Wept thorough,
Your bleeding eyes

Growing more hoarse-
Screaming a name.

We shared a picnic blanket
In fields
Where these hypnotic contests
Raged
The boundaries of our bed,
Our anguish,
Different thorns
A rose dyed stain.
Still…
It carries no blade
Often walks without notice
Or care
Carries on,
Without shame.
Then when it finds you lost
Embraced by it,
You ran away?

What choices have we made to become so afraid?

Our voices spiraling…
In the whirlwinds of a noiseless hurricanes
When you forget me.
Erase
What little,
My voice proclaims.
From the tattered edges of picture
Cast off our star-crossed flames!
Muttered on only as something
You've lost-
Or perhaps misplaced.

Another withering spark,
Upon eternity's face.
Living on knowing
Our thorns carved different
But cut
All the same

Lost in smoke
There are no hours.
The second time spent,
Washed down bloody drains,
There, showered.
Juvenile budding flowers.
Their scent still lingering
Washed away laments
Sensations that devoured.
What little remains of emotions,
Now sour.
All I held in silver
Gold and green,
Reflected on rippled water seams
Soaking fingers,
Stained black and unclean
Perhaps it's soot,
Or pyroclast?
From a pipe's murky glass,
I licked clean.
Smiling yellow as eyes,
Turned a glossy sheen.
Unaware now of the hours,
Passing in between.
Smoking for sake of breath
Is what it seems
Not what it was meant,
To have been.

Lost in smoke
There are no hours.

Only withered petals,
And burning tree.

The Drowning Sea

Living
So, it would seem
While sirens sing over
Surf warped rocks
I sail into an expanding green sea
Navigating through vengeful waves
A quest behind questions,
Of what to be?
Each shore,
Each wave,
The horizon slips,
To rogue waves
Cracking apart vessels,
Under siege.
At the helm
I away and watch
Bound to the deck
The icy waters foam
Touching my knees
And yet I could not see!
To my questions
What I sought,
What calls to me,
Swallow!
The drowning sea!

There's beauty in madness
Strength instilled in sorrow,

All I wanted to say
In the mirror
I practiced
We scheduled for seven…
Then eleven…
By afternoon,
I knew it wasn't gonna be soon
You don't seek anything
That isn't within you
But by this time tomorrow
The boy kept waiting
For a man he never knew
Tried to find something else
To balm the burns
And empty words
Inflicted by you
There's beauty in the madness
And strength instilled in sorrow
But each day
You left me waiting
Voiceless whispers
Came baying

'I never wanted you'

Blackpool's Charade

What troublesome wind,
Howls along this pathway
Come shrieking down
The Mountain's uneven crown.
Who walks there,
Among winding roads?
Leaving prints and pebbles,
To elucidate in clay
What fallen crests
And angel nests
Lay scattered,
Down in the bay?
Take me now...
From that sunless cavern
Down!
Through wood's entrails away!
To sit with frothy mugs,
Grasped tight in hand,
Of a ruddy tavern
Humming the beguiled melodies
Songs of golden yester and roaring to-days!
What ruckus came roaring-
Came rising from the Mountain's valley!
Would this be?
This melody that beckons
Which carried you,
To recline,
In the early hours
Restless afternoons haze

Or shall I find another bed,
In which to lay?
For praying,
Wasn't enough foreplay
Our love to stay,
Uncorroded
Without a single hair,
Greyed
So that I may find rest
Among old nocturnes
In a welcomed array
Till we meet again
In that musty tavern
Where laughter resonates
Upon the same breeze willows sway
And our fears,
Oh,
Those troublesome taxes paid!
Now all but flown away.
We share our drinks,
Our smiles,
Our undaunted old ways.
No more than memoirs
Humbled
"Good days!"
Rolling freely
Across mumbling,
Hickory waves
Sunlight woven into dressing gowns
How her lips curled in such a way
That our youth filled me with brilliance,

Everlasting play,
As stars in,
Blackpool's charade
Now resting proudly
Carried in mists
That which crown the mountain grey
While I remain.
Listening to howling winds
Come down
To be whisked away
In a few drinks
To life's final praise!

Clouds of the morning breeze.
What muffled chirps serenade me?
Resting on budding branches.
Each petal unfolding a vision.
Building castles and piercing towers.
Washing away the minutes
Who built hours?
Foolish men,
Brought onto to their knees.
Plaguing desires.
Discover-
Each breath taken within
Dazzling
A Harmonious spark
Become eternity.

I dare not kiss the sunrise
My lips would writhe and wilt
Like so many flowers laying at the roadside
Her love,
A lingering herbicide

What's more depressing?
    The graceless dead,
    Or pressed flowers
    Between pages unread?

Personally, I'd climb the ladder
    If only to ascend and lay
    In the curled knots
    Of a sweat stained
    Bedspreads.

What's more depressing?
    The linger of verse
    Whispered between
    Empty sheets.

Wrapped in her scent,
    Within hours
    Without end?

Or that you'll never hear
    the hedonic breaths
    of her moans again?

Blurred
Calloused fingertips,
   Tracing crimson
   Chapped lips

A stolen sanguine kiss,
   A taste of iron
   I can't replace

Cigarettes embers,
   Pressing cherries
   Into pale skin

I begin to resurrect,
   Old names and
   And flames displaced

While counting constellations,
   Her freckles
   Make the scene

A blurred face

Adhesion

Another cut isn't enough
Remind us
Of our commonplace
Blood in a blushing
Face
Or that we all bleed
Regardless
Of the sanctity
You chase

A journeyman's curse,
Paints runic hymns
Across unsettled bones
He couldn't find rest
He walks down between
Towns without names
Roads without ends
Finding no sleep
From rasping breath,
Of disparaged saints.
Weeping in their windows
Their voices muddled
By grated,
Savin moans.
What little bits and bobs,
A Traipsing trail.
Of Fractured glass,
Across spattered stone.
He'll wander nameless
Cursed by hymns
Restless by their bones.

The Sun's setting nears
Call to my brothers and sisters
Tell them I'm near
To where jade water sways,
In evening's soft whisper.
Gathering the grinning loners,
The loving sinners,
Us miserable drifters.
Sharing in songs
Of roadside misadventures
Yellow keys feigning notes
Retiring tears
Into forgetful hours
On the brink of mourning
Their shadows shall find shade
Without farewell,
And long heartfelt goodbyes
None meant to impress
Or long to stay.
Semblance of spirits laughing
Ghostly countenances will fade
Silhouettes dancing
Above the waves
Beyond the bay
All but gone
Their souls
Drifting above
Winter's silent grace,
What's become of our longing?
Chances to chase,
The unknown paths,

We take.
Gone now
Neither our footprints
Or the melodies
Born out of warmer days
Chlorophyll hearts
No longer beating
Near to this
Pale terrace
Only gentle laughter
My mind falters
I begin to ask
What will come after
This last memory...
When I wake

I sought a home
From far below
Rusted hinges
Holding doors
I Sought to close.
Hide myself,
amongst the stone.
So young and cold.
The pieces never shone
Trying to run blind!
Down a country road
Now I know
That the home sought from,
The below
Was in a heart
Tightly closed
To be alone
That's what I chose

Reap all that's sown!

Now exposed
The whisper of the winds
Giggles rustling
Shivering trees.
Fallen on bloodied knees
Like rain pattering
Upon mossy stones
The paths Id lost
Those crooked roads
Were leading me here

To build my home

It was a gray morning
I sat on the porch smoking Champagne.
Playing with the smoke coiled around my neck.
Fashioning rings between my fingers
With deep and focused breath.
You packed your things and headed towards the
door.
Throwing as many pictures in your wake
As your folded hands could carry.
Bits of glass scatter under bare feet
Leaving dark water streaming along
Wood panel floors.
Tripping on all the empty promises said
But meant
"for sure."
Falling harder than early morning rain.
You lay there begging for strength
Thin whispers summoned prayers.
In the silence of our house, you plead
"I can't take this anymore!"
"Let me out!'
Into the empty space
Of an opened door.

I said I was 'Alright'
Small truths
Bled from archaic lines
There's no easy phrase
Or way to describe
You go through the day
Disguised
Each smile is a mask
Each breath a task
When you ask
How I am
And I say 'alright'
Don't be surprised
If you wake up tomorrow
I never told you a lie
It's not that you're blind
Because what I said
Was 'I'm Alright'
What I meant was
"I'm tired of being alive."

The bills are piling up
You were late to work
It felt so hard to breath
Like you'd been choking
Without a right to live,
Your own life
Sometimes you'd drink
One or two was okay
Once the bottle was empty
You filled it with spite
Stumbling through the hall
You heard a knock at the door
Welcoming with open arms,
The faceless night.
Beneath black skies,
With neither roof nor floor
You tripped on the knots
Of tree roots winding
The forest floor
A bruise grew over your eye
Your chest felt sore
At once you found it
No longer pissed
Or lost in the traipsing
Of a senseless stupor
All of it
The Hate
The anger
the desires-
What we call 'more'
All your woven stains

Washed away
In the embrace
Of the compassionate rain

After a terrible storm
You became weightless
On the journey home
They could listen
but they didn't hear you
They watched
but they couldn't see you
They could take hold
but they couldn't feel
As you were just a phantom-
A passing glimpse
Your own shadow
Staining the corner of their eyes
drifting seamlessly
from one room to the next
Never knowing
How to rest
Only an inconsolable dread
Harboring the sensations
Of being hollow
Held within bloody threads

Trying hard to peer through stars
I imagined I could encapsulate all of space
What decisions remained
came a vision of what I need to face
To give into trust of my senses
to smell and listen
or to categorize all on which
We are based
Finding myself swallowed
By the drops of a bottle
Fallen asleep in the gutters of a grotto
Questioning if all these
Bladeless wounds
Would close out tomorrow
Until I awoke and replaced
My hanging disgrace
Finding my chest was little more
Than empty space
There were no words
No colors
Or a name
A canvas bled across
Became plain
I wandered in the dark
Sang in moonlight
Caught stars like fireflies
Late into the night
And what little sights I held
I recorded with haste
Finding myself was
Silently displaced

What once was 'I'
wanted to be erased
Now to run and chase
Until I lastly retire
Welcoming a breath
With her gentle embrace
Summer come to me
With fresh taste

The song of cicadas and the way sweat tastes.
The warm breeze pushing leaves like ocean waves.
Sometimes I stop and I just stare.
There wasn't anything particular
I just wanted to be there.
In a moment I found
A strange sense of peace.
What's more calming than listening to the breeze.
I wonder if it could see and speak.
What sort of worldly secrets?
It might lay at my feet.
Maybe If I could return as the breeze.
I'd forever retain the rhythm
Of the dancing of trees.
And the freedom of falling leaves.

I saw within
Burning my chest
Mistaken as my heart
I 'was'
For a moment
My mind felt clear
As the crystal waters
Rippling beneath the pier
So warm
I melted in its warmth
Until I disappeared
Auburn petals
Soaking sand
A flurry of sparks and embers
I could not withstand
I saw it
As If I observed from afar
I was staring into the sky
Seeing a single shimmering star

Still waters run deep and cool
Even spilt on the bathroom floor
The blood boils in a pool without depth
I wish I wasn't so unimpressed
by just how many times
You can cut a wrist
Or choke on your breath
And still be up for work on time
Smiling and laughing
as you pull on your sleeves
Hoping no one sees it
Tries to peer into the deep
Remember the first time
standing before the sea
In awe of each crashing and rolling wave
Wondering with a nagging anxiety
Of what nightmares lurk just beneath
Scared by the thing you'll see
Even if you only wanted a peak
Paralyzed before the monsters that lurk beneath
Still waters running deep

'Come home-'
I saw it but didn't bother
To count.
How many hours had passed?
Since I read the message,
Last.
Or how many of those murky memories
Came rushing through my mind?
As the moments frozen
Brush marked flesh.
The breeze of swaying Elysian fields
Skin now healed.
At what point did I realize?
For I who still haunts,
Clutching to lingering memories,
Past.
Finding no solace
In her's or mine
Laughter.
What was ours?
What will come to pass?
All of us
Captured in a message,
Last.
'It's late.'
'So come home dumbass.'

The kind of guy
Taking late night drives
Blasting Pearl Jam through
Bass boosted speakers
On his feet torn
Nike sneakers
Eyes closing
Driving alone
Worn them out running from,
Empty promises.
Muttering back to himself,
Those sweetly honied lies.
Salt coating chapped lips.
Rain clouds stirring
Behind closed eyes.
Swerving on through lightless hills
Beneath star coated skies
Not afraid as the wheel turns
White smoke filling the street
Letting out a heart stalling screech
With no one around
Did it make a sound?
When parted lips whisper
'Goodbye.'
Did it resound?
Or like falling trees in the woods.
Did he make any sound?
Or lay silent on the mound…

A toast for the last of us here
Unhindered,
I say no cheers are held by fear
Except for those who no longer become riled
By burning wood piles, we danced around
Calling to desire
The night growing ever brighter by the pyres
A drink for those who stood where others knelt.
Who did not shy from the stinging wounds,
They were dealt.
We drink to remind ourselves.
Of those we have loved so well.
Journeying on...
Those who have given themselves to winds and
set sail.
Swelled are the hearts on foamy shores
Waving to them goodbye,
Farewell!
So drink my friends as you will.
Emptied cups may always be refilled.
In these halls where we reminisce
let old songs from your tongues roll.
Laugh as the warmth grows
Times continues to pass.
So drink my brothers, My sisters!
My fathers and mothers!
Share their embrace,
Another beloved!
Drink for the hours
shall soon eclipse.
Sunlight on the mast

Of ceremony's carven ships!
Come calling us from home,
To lands beyond,
Where we must roam.
Saying our farewells to friends
For tonight is not an end
Tomorrow another sun rises!
We shall share our drinks
Again.

Goodbye is what I wanted to say
To let slip my vulnerability
But the words would not form
From my parted lips
Like the exhaled smoke that twirls
They soon faded
And here I lay in silence
A darkened ceiling was welcoming me
To the maw of my grave
Goodbye to be the last words
To settle a heart,
Swayed.
But truth found on lies
Could never be expressed properly
And here I lay
Waiting
Watching
Hiding.
From light's first break.
From one God or another's,
Ruinous pathways.
Unable to form those words on my lips
Before the dawn gives way.
Instead,
I'm going to fall asleep once more,
Afraid.

No flames emit light in this space.
No candles or matches are struck.
What quiet prayers are whispered,
Hold no grace.
A tenderness of fingers
Drawing along black lace.
She humming some faint familiar tune
A mysterious melody
I had yet exhumed
The warm roll of her laughter
Thereafter
Reminding me of tangled sheets,
I'd once smoothed.

There is no warmth in place.

Only blurred visions of his gaze
Enveloped where once crackling flames
Laid waste
Photos and crumpled paper turning to ashes
The grayed cinders purged away the sensation
There lingered.
From love's intoxicating taste,
Anger, Replaced.
A grin dares not make the mistake of,
Exposure to coy smoldering eyes,
Willingly delved into.
Yet if the sea is wide
All the more lost
are those,
The ones who dared to explore

The wave's smooth curves
Far and un-abiding.
Tasting the fresh lotus flowers
and bare fruits,
Dawning a freshly tailored suit.
Whispers of conversations over candlelight.
Who sits in that dinner chair tonight?
Who holds her hand and strokes her fingers,
So gingerly?
Unaware of the thirst behind Hazelnut eyes.
That night she never even said goodbye
Only that which is loved is met by heartfelt goodbyes.
Laying in tangled sheets I whisper.
Her love was by far the best of her lies

We loved
We craved
Holding each other tight
In the nights that dragged
A cigarette dying fame
In the early morning rays
In the embers falling grace
She felt encased
I couldn't feel more distance
How far my thoughts raced
And she raced to meet me there
To say
'My love'
'You don't seem well these days'
I knew it true but could not say
Love was something
My calloused fingers never touched
A calcified tongue could not taste
Wasted on a park bench
A hoarse voice tries to lament
What little blurred thoughts he collects
Forever a sinner without a voice
To rise and rise like a melancholy choir
Unable to repent
The venomous bite
Of an uncoiled serpent

The petals remained
A stem that withstood winds,
Of the storm which reigned
She was like the flower I saw that day
Watching from behind the battered windowpane
Nothing I could have said
Would take that pain
Nothing from my lips would cast it astray
I remained composed,
Silent.
Watching petals dripped with drops
Of rain.
Each new bloom in never quite the same
Yet all the same,
The flower
Through the storm can remain
"Beautiful."
Would an unconcerned mind say the same?
I'm not sure.
Am I concerned?
I can only pronounce metaphors
To explain what could and could not be gained.
Like plucked flowers
a heart stolen
A stem fragile as the glass
Like the glass reflecting winter's eyes
Thick with disdain.
Innocence stolen
Never again was that bed
Made the same
Like trampled flowers

Petals blood stained

On some distant shore
The tide will recede exposing,
What the sea left behind.
It's there I will build.
Wandering between the sharpened rocks
And forgotten seashells
With my hands clutching dust.
I will fashion a castle of sand.
Taking torches, I shall mount the walls
Dressing ever darkened towers
With reverberating firelight
And fashion the golden grains into glass.
Where nothing is hidden in my halls.
Except the past.
Carefully I buried you
Beneath the rolling plains of grass.
On a shimmering throne
Before the crystal court
My fingers shall strum chords
And David shall become my name
Ignore the pleading calls
The hooked strings dragging me towards
A place I have brashly called home
Here I will rest and remain
Until another tide rushes to bury
Or carry my crystal keep
Far from this empty place
If my walls are too weak
And crumble back into the sea
I shall keep moving forward
Whatever it takes

I wanted to find happiness
Just a sip of ambrosia
Inhale burning leaves
The smell turning heads
At times fiends
Wanderers looking through wastelands
for a tribe and to chief
But the body consuming became meager
It's tightened grip,
Weak
Unable to speak further to those who indulge
The fears and thoughts unsafe,
I'd keep
Hoarded and stored until the bottle
couldn't retain its shape anymore
Lost in the senselessness of the morphine
I have engorged
Tasting the nectar was so bittersweet
My mind left unchecked,
Shattered into reflected pieces
Scattered like that whisky bottle,
We whipped down
a darkened street
The heavy musk of vodka on trembling lips
Laughing hard
a breath was harsh to keep
Eyes wet
tasting far more sweet
Than the burning streams
running down my cheeks

Tonight
'Another sip' I whisper
'I'll be just right'
Content in misery's
beautifully warped sheets
A trapped soul in its mortal coils
Will transcended
This tired heading
become dim as church candlelight
Was it worth it?
to fight and fight
Until no more blood
could be spilled
Another mad man
cries out to the moon
God is dead! God is dead!
Does he still hear me
My tragic prayers in Seraphim spite!
No I think not
And the hour is late
So I shall stumble and crawl
under yellow sheets
Ever peaceful in the gentle cradle
To sleep
...Friends,
Goodnight

He asked me "If you had three wishes what would they be?"

"Enough money to travel."

"What else?"

"Maybe an island all my own."

"The last wish?"

"To fly."

"That's interesting."

"What?" I asked.

"You didn't wish to be rid of the depression."

I can try and explain
But the words on these
crumpled pages stained
Cannot express what it feels like
To lose what felt right
Letting loose the clasped fingers,
So tight
And descend into sheets undressed
Sobbing into
The sweat stained pillows
As if you'd become possessed
I was possessed
In drenched dreams
Id thrash
Blankets and pillows
laying across my floor
And for all the water poured
between chapped lips
Only in those malleable bottles
I felt refreshed
A leash to the lash
An escape from the past
Everything I was trying to build
Falling like burning mountain ash
The more I poured into the fire
My lungs filling with soot and choked
Plastic desire
Washing the debris ashore
Laying in the sand the tide rolls back
My footprints disappear at last

People will go through life thinking
a paper will carry them there
That place they desire to go
The idea that a diploma
is the end of the road
There's no more worry
once the books are closed
Their pencils are left
beside the desks
Classrooms doors
Locked and closed
I was always anxious in school yards and desk
chairs
Nervous before
The bored and wandering,
Empty stares
Slowly I was walking to the truth
life isn't always fair
Despite this I've still been able to carry myself
down the stairs
To counter and high tops
The smell of steamed milk
Coffee mixed in cream
Wiping off tables
Embracing an addicts irritated
Glare
They don't care,
So you learn quick,
Not to mind.
A few more hours to go
I'll walk back home

In the steady desk lamp glow
I'll grind pencil to paper
Prepare tea on the stove
Miles away
a painter stains their sleeves
A mural there
is shown
It didn't matter whether or not
it was a classroom they chose
School was one path of many
To follow
Sometimes
It's just another step down the road

When I go don't pray for me
Sadly,
We never could see eye to eye
So as I close mine
I'll smile
To greet you one last time
Where the new shores will curl around,
White sands
Before the violet crown of dusk
or the sunrise
Turning pink as you rest your weary legs
In the sand beside mine
At last open
what was crystalized
And behold the new world
Breath in all that is yours
If the heart is truly the home
Then together we'll walk on forever
Laughing and running
as if our muscles and bones
Had never grown old
To adventure into
The next lands unknown
Unbeknownst to those
safely gathered
Whispering in silent remembrance
the lord's poems
Sadly,
We never saw eye to eye
With my last breath
my only prayer will be

One day they see this new Sun,
And I'll rise
Free and uncrystallized

Late Night Texts

I haven't been sober since May
I'm starting to forget even my day to day
When was the last time I spoke to my friends
'Is even important anymore?'
To ask about their weekend
'Would I care even if I asked?'
So much of what I remember about them
A couple years past
I'm starting to slip more
Knocking my Tv onto the books
on my bedroom floor
Trippin on shoes
I met the table corner
Barely noticing a scar
until I found blood on my
Bathroom floor
What's this warmth?
I've never felt it before
My clothes stink
It's puke I think
What were these bandages for?

Right, I fell...

I've been that drunk before
Greeting the ground
with my head
My fingers
reach out to the bottle

I'd finished tens of times before
My body shaking in anticipation
Give us more
Until we're so spun
we can't think anymore
Or harass old flames
Floated towards southern shores
Why am I this way?
Whose idea was this tragic face?
Never mind...
another drink will put me in a better place
I've given up on finding one
A hare took some Adderall
while a drunk prefers
The turtle's race
 Or is that just a common mistake
Telling myself this behavior is commonplace

        If only for a moment I could return to that
shore
        Right before my hand graces the door
        I'll whisper to that unsullied hide
        'It's not worth it son, what're you're searching
for, isn't inside the liquor store.'
        No bottle is going to fill you enough to-
            No liquid is kind enough to let you confide
            Only to let what's strangling you hide
            Until you're too sedated to meet it
            It'll twist your heart and mind
            Stupor, thy name shall be mine
            Is that drink worth the lost time?

Tell me when you were full of drink
Did you feel any more fulfilled inside?

Unseen

I like those who have storms
Brewing inside
Stirring up mischief
Behind a curved smile
Who like to dance in the rain
Aren't afraid to expose
A mind more wild
than sane
Laughing dancing and singing
Through the sun and rain
Unhindered by the sculpture's scars
Dragged grooves along porcelain
The alluring madness melded
By welcoming what others might

Have left unseen

I apologize
These days have gone by so quickly
I've failed to give a proper goodbye
What murky visions that I stole from my memory
Show only the summary of a campfire
And a missed sunrise
How many more nights will I survive
Hiding inside these sensations
Something I can't seem to say
but use to disguise
In the flurry of stained sheets
My ears brimming with terrible whispers
Tears welling to crusted eyes
I'm sorry you must hear these cries
Laying here zombified
The dead is stirring tonight
as his is sadness
Is at last satiated
My thoughts drawing more to finding
A greater height
A single step and I'll taste the breeze
Unnoticed the witness to the lamps in the street
One fading as you pass by

Carnival

Run the world like a carnival
Eating with freaks like hungry cannibals
What flesh betrays,
The heart still opened in surgery-
Beats away!
From the stage we'll watch
As the fire consumes,
The lion's mane
Dance bearded lady dance
Danse Macabre!
Until the curtains fall
And we fail in our passion's
Devouring embrace
And devour him and all he holds
Become one in the single mold
A twisted set of limbs and stunted bones
Gurgle as you stumble across the circus tent floor
Dragging behind a trail of blood or tattered cloth
The crowd laughs and hoots
Their empty gazes mute
before the show of freaks
Ready to scrape their spare coins and loot
They'll cast them from their hands
to your boots
Grovel!
Grovel common man seated in bleachers
Clapping uncalloused hands
Your grin so wide
it near splits the cheeks

What sort of faculties does the common man
keep?
Wandering in and out of gin and vodka stupor
What sort of secrets does the freak reap?
Hoping curled fingers
might stain themselves sooner
The line to the table is long
as the ringmaster's baton
Beating the freaks along the stage
While children laugh and their fingers
Point in disarray
The curtain falls
stamped split kernels
Are soon brushed away
Freaks resting in drafty boxcars
Grinning at the paper gathered today
Unafraid of the common man
His own freakishness
Afraid to display

The universe likes to laugh and play with you.

It gets easier if you learn to laugh too.

Tomorrow

I was sheltered by glass
Watching warped images
dance from behind.
Each swan's neck I'd throttled
Content in the celebration
of an unforgiving tomorrow
For each gulp and sip
For each cancer stick and spliff
I faded further from warped images
Behind the thickening glass
of the prison
If the poison in my breath
were to tame me tomorrow
I'd spend one last night
smashing every bottle
And wretch back every drop
I'd swallowed
If only to punish myself,
Running from tomorrow

Three sheets to the wind
Giggling
Red cheeks
slick with grease
Indulging the carousel swirl
The rooms' dancing
No music anymore
Only orphaned
dusty strings
Sure, were to I to pluck
A vengeful snap
at the final pass
Of my fingertips to their
Reverberant murmuring
I once went along
just to sing
What sort of sonnets
can you bring
From a dead man
Telling tales
Composing his final lament
Out a sunken treasure chest
Tipped funny on its side
The S.S. Intrepid
Docked in
An ocean trench
Their songs
Gone
Gone three sheets to the wind
Cradle by the storm
It's castaways

Become little more than empty
Coffee mugs
Their words left afloat
In murky bottles in the
Emerald shallows
of the sea
Uncorked laughing
so joyously
The sort of laughter
madness found
coursing through the breeze
Admiring the spinning whirlpools
of adventurous uncertainty
Accompanied by the subtle taste of salt
On pursed lips
those bottles
Tipped back
Drowned ourselves
before the ship went in
Gone
Three sheets to the wind

"Where is the path?"
I do not know
"I'm looking at the stars"
"Where are you?"
The sun rises
Towing myself out of bed
Readying for the day's punch card
Drawing the blinds closed
I button my shirt and draw on my pants
"Mustn't forget to eat again"
Look in the mirror
Wash your hands
Spark the lighter
"Dammit I forgot to eat again"
Drive to work
smile
Laugh
A long sigh before saying 'bye'
"How was your day?

"Fine."

"Just fine?"
"Yeah."
"You don't say much anymore."
"What's there to say?"
I eat and feel emptier than before
Maybe I'll force it out
before I lay down
"Anything at all."
"I'm fine."

I lied
That's fine
Right?

I think of my mother
Who would sit up and ponder
The lonely night
For when the birds are silent
And the dawn
yet to arrive
What sort of darkness
might have befallen
Gazing into sunset eyes
Would she weep for the boy?
Or be proud of the man?
In rumpled sheets would she want to hear
My boisterous laughter again?
Please don't shed many tears
May the warmth of your memories
Drive off the burdensome fears
For I think of you before many others
To why I stayed here
And when those twisted creatures
Coming crawling into the night
Or beneath the sun
Your sun
Remains and sits
Forever raging against
The dying lights

If you believe
It's just a phase
Perhaps that's all it is
Perhaps the one who convinced you
Was full of shit
Remember the moon
goes through phases
And it's more beautiful
When it shines at night
Isn't it?

Father
Where have you gone?
Why do these marble walls
No longer resonate Sera's song?
Why did you leave my side
Letting all our treasured shells
Flow beneath the evening tide
Tell me and I will ask of you
What lies in a past no longer viewed?
The streaming sobs of a boy
Left to ponder what all this emptiness
Is meant to mean

Hollowness it seems

I was destined to wander the shore
Mumbling of choirs and
I miss the lullabies she'd sing
All the same Father
You no longer fill my dreams
I've found Sera
At the edge of a stream
Her clothes soaked
Held to her skin
Clasping an empty bottle in her hand
I found no message
Kneeling in the burning sands
Only a whisper
Making my eyes well
Bleeding with silver
My breath stunk with the poison

That had felled her
And together we drifted
Beneath the sea
"Why couldn't you love me?"

Spirit frail as linen
With distraught sisters
Eyeing tangled
Red strings
Whispering of what's to be
and unknowable things
Yet a single eye
given before the tree
Where deaf men find music
By patience breath
Wistfully running bone thin fingers
Coated in silver

"All is well!"

The preacher man said
While the gallows hum lowly
The breeze running through
Matted strands of black hair
His throat tearing
With crimson seams
Grinning wide
as those do
Who dream wild dreams
Lost in the entrails
Of a painted mind
Unveiled secrets
Of distraught sisters
Playing with
Crimson strings

Blasting furious songs
To help us move on
Numbing any lingering feelings
From drags out the bowl of a bong
And who the fuck left the clocktower on!
The same sound that gave me hope
To look in the mirror with red eyes
Whispering to myself
"I wasn't in the wrong"
But once the bowls are scraped
And the company fucked off
Yes!
They are gone!
There is only a haunting silence
I am withdrawn
Reclining into the back of my mind
Where the hungry shadows
Stumbling out from where
The blinds are drawn
Mistaken for
Dear friends
The shadows
Born from the Clock-tower's
Chime

You're wise to bask in the warm sunlight
Do not fall prey to the words of
Defeated minds
Autonomous minds
Whose efforts only turn
Old dials
Replacing rusty cogs
Breathing no steam
Become an oddity and splash color
On blank canvas,
Display yourself
Others may witness your wonders,
And too,
Follow down curious and winding
Pathways
Go forth and dive
Under great waves of thought
Create new inspired ways
to bring change
Fend of this great malaise
Society's decay
The modern become dulled
Convenience turned children slaves
Take hold the brush,
the pen,
the strings,
And play!
Play through nights into days
Play until trending greys
fade away
Play!

Learn to love the brilliant colors
Only *your* heart can display

There is no bracelet
Or pendent around my neck
I've forsaken my kind symbols
For the taste of lighter fluid
On my breath
All that remains is the darkened face
Of my dear teacher
On the littlest finger
he rests
Watching calmly
without judgement
His stilled features
bring forth wisdom yet
The buddha is calm
Like petals floating on water
Undisturbed by dark clouds
Gathering within my mind
Stirring waves to rise
Winds blowing across
Encroaching prairies
Letting old embers
Take flight
Once more the night
Shall be auburn bright
And scorched will be
these forgotten lands
Reaching far to the ocean's edge
Alone
I stand
Clutching his ring
within the palm of my hand

New petals unfold
From the drops
Fallen on the sand

There are no right words
Or copied lyrics
To display,
How I'd want to tell you-
After all the pages
You've touched
And the words and phrases
That touched you
Have any held you gently by the hand?
Have any whispered your fears away?
On those darkened nights
Sat down
Beside your bed
Unsure you breathe softly
Full of dreams
Of warm summer rays
And shady trees
Swaying in the breeze
Hearing a voice from a thousand miles away
Whispering
"It's going to be okay"
Sleep now and rise to the new day
A phoenix rises from the ashes
In which it lays

Oh, we so equally view each other?
Eventually the sadder man
Might pulls his fingers
around the strings
Close the shutter
What is a world that welcomes one another?
When ten countries away
A bullet pierces a man's brother
Please give me your sermons and soliloquies
Throw me down
Before the goblet of sanctity
With the waters of the martyr
Drink with me!
Let me show you then
Why there is no gospel
Written upon bended knees
Brand me
And my word be a plague
For a plague was beyond reason
A reason to change
I'd gladly stumble
Weighed down by chains
I name them
Reason.
Change.
And for those who watch the dead man swing
"Do the giants care for what the small men sing?"
There's a song in my head
A knife through the heart
I've walked this road before
But where did it start?

Did I build myself up
To be torn back apart?
When all the lyrics are sung
And my journey almost done
Is the end of my road
The bang of a drum?
To silence the noise
Locked in my head
Or forgotten
With unsung dead
Will I be sent
Down in the yard
Of the dried riverbed

Selfcare should rise
Above all other things
An unhealthy mind
IS a disease
So please
Take time to get away
And let yourself be unwound
From the tiresome things
Work yes
To earn comfort and food
But take ease in parts,
Too
Your mind may become
like an abandoned well
You, laying in its depths
Forever cold
Staring up into a distant light
Without rope.
Without wings.
A tired crane
Taking no flight
You're still shoulder it
But trust me
Things will unfold
Each day is a breath
Slowly taken
Even after you quit drinking
You'll find your hands
May not stop shaking
But find them steady,
In their motion

So when you're by yourself
In this Un-Well
Strangled by the anxious commotion
Telling yourself
It's better to reside in hell
I will reach in and shake you
You are royalty
Not some frog
Stuck in a well

Others can't tell you
How to live your life
They can't tell you how
To stand up straight
You're gonna have to learn
to identify those traits
Through fire
Through stalling waters
The tears that flow
Hidden
Down shower grates
And all those pages
Inked by your pain
You sought to display
To chase Sorrow away
If I could rid you of them
I would
It'd be foolish of me to say
I stood
where you've stood
The demons I faced
Have taught me
How it's easy
For a heart to burn
Like dry wood
Sometimes mistaken by passion
But fingers tied,
Aren't asking forgiveness
Has brought me no closer
To god's selective good
Than running away

To find
Spirits dancing in the woods
Take your time
Take a breath
For the sake of yourself
Go to bed and rest

Your ridges and scars
Are beautiful
They have made you
who you are
You dazzling
Work of art

Sit down my friend
Some tea?
Tell me of your adventures.
And all the mysterious places,
You've been.
Of damp and misty woods
And the windy valley glens
Tell me where your off to next
When will you wander backwards again?
Lead me down the trail of memories
Of dreams
Trace with your finger
The constellations,
You've seen
Tell me of all the wonders,
In between
Here and back
Fellow wanderer
Your stories
I want to sing of them

You're not lost
You just haven't discovered yourself yet

Wander on my friend
I'll be here when you get back

I feel older than I am somedays
Not in a mature way
Only that I've become more weary
As if my bones and mind
Are soon to decay

Who am I to say,
What is wrong?
What stands justifiably right?
What speeches
Words of wisdom
I've listened.
Burdensome words
Of another playwright
Passed gingerly between
Sheets of laminated paper
Lamented in yellow lamplight
Branded across the stretched skin.
Who am I to say?
That games played
Are any more fun
Than watching dogs run
How I envy
The playful nature of animals
Who roll is the grass and tails wag
While I sit transparent
Gray by the smoke
Of cigarette drags
Plagued by the thought that,
I may read ten thousand words
Quote a hundred works
To you
And still
Cannot find the right words
To say

I feel as though I speak a different language
That I am a stranger
Who cannot explain
I try hard to speak
But they stare at me blank
I turn the pages
Run my fingers
I show the images
Recite the words!
Still I feel only silence
Was I too eager?
My mind too absurd?
What is it I lack,
To be heard.

The Road Is Rough the Grass Is Soft

I took flight
And floated between stars
To find out what I am
What we really are
In the vast wandering
My mind began to drift
Soon it felt as though
I didn't really exist
The lights began to fade
Everything was falling away
There!
Caged in the cold emptiness
My intent was to remain
To be displaced
From all things
I'd been touched by
Faintly in the distance
A warm voice whispered
"You're going to be okay"

I'll wake up tomorrow
To repeat those words to myself
I can keep walking forward
Whispering in the same way

Today, I'm going to be okay.

To the Ones Left Behind

Doing fine
A little more out of my mind
But that's no different from then
We'd listen to those familiar rhymes
You'd play a track and smith your own
On those late-night car rides
I sat silent
Bobbed my head and listened
Afraid of what I'd say
Afraid I'd look like a fool
My silence
was an agreement
With my own self inflicted
Violence
When I left
I promised I'd return
And said all my goodbyes
But that just wasn't true
It was the end of time
And the greatest fault is believing
Nothing ever ends
Because saying you'd come back
After a goodbye
Is a double edged lie

To have passion
How could you not?
To stride forward
With all you've got
To climb a mountain
To swim in seas of thought
Going against the grain
And finding all the pearls
You've wrought
Tell me of passion
Show you're plight
Charging forward,
Into the night
Streaming like comets and meteors
Burning bright
See how far you'll travel
Provoked you've learned
To take fight
Taste the waters so fresh
It nourishes a tender soul
Drowned out spite
Grow vines on walls
So humanity knows
Even across cold stones
Life flourishes
And grows
Tell me the secrets of the world
Only you know
Teach them
The magic of your grace
And above all

Be bold
For all that glitters
May not be gold
For you,
Who shines brighter
Than any star
I'll behold

There's nothing more noble
Than trying to create
To take paints and pens
Running theme across cavern
And canvas
Rounding circles of phrases
And words floating
Like the feathers of birds
To make the head spin
The heart open
Look to the branches of trees
The rocks under leaves
Stare at the stars
Sing in locked cars
Lay in the sun
Dance to the beat of thunder
The world is singing
Just as you are
Breathing
Sit beside me
Tell me
Of other worlds you've seen
Of monsters and Heroes
of lovers
And musicians
Bend me a melody
from golden strings
Slide the brush
Create an open sea
Let the blood boil
In deep thought

Fill your rivers
Become more
Than just another light
Burning dimmer
Burn bright and beautiful
As stars and planets
Across a black canvas
Glimmer
Guiding us through the night
See sailors had it right
Making maps and charts of the sky
To have it rest in your eyes
Every night
They'll be waiting
To see you out there
Nothing is sweeter
When inside strangers
An artist appears

The spark of a match
Laid to the packed
Baci
Stirred by fire to raise
A plume into the patient lungs
Exhale the breath
And the cloud soon fades
Like all things expanding
It rolls like ripples
On the pond
Floating clouds
On the horizon
Painted pink and orange
By the setting sun
After the buzz
What sensations remain?
What memory will remain
Of this dusty place?
The song of robins
And mourning doves
They remember their nest
when no trees are left
Will the doe still graze these
Abandoned pastures
These hills that have grown silent
The people are gone
Their fires that no longer burn
Merely a moment ago
I heard their muffled cheers
An echo of laughter
Merely a breath and the moment passes

Unheard

All things in time fade
Ever more so left
Undisturbed
Soon the sun will set
And so shall the memory
Of the day
A single breath was enough
And not another word

Grimoires

This shall be my new salvation
Liberty,
Freed with the ecstasy of
Robbed words
Hidden intent
The sweet vines to ferment
Docile minds and parlor tricks
The idea of which none of us
Have it
Dance and sing from the towers of old
Watch the senile be freed
The youngsters never to taste
Dusts and molds
For the liberation of their morals
From the shackles of-
Hand cupped molds
Will shatter like clay
Across the tavern floor
Within these pages
I find my salvation
Free to lay with angels
And taunt their democratic
Proclamations
So let your wings unfold
Your hands rise
Tonight we dine and forsake
All that which were taught
To behold
As children

These golden shackles
A prison for the mind!

What's the first philosophy
Ya ever got fueled with?
A generator kept you going through
A winter of thoughts
Late at night
You'd sit up with their words
Staring out the frosted window
The other side of the pane
Still and undisturbed
What poet gave you kindred warmth
Who filled you
Verse that stirred you
Made your heart rev and pound
A storm yet unobserved
What new ones have you learned?
What depths have you searched?
What rocks upturned?
What songs rest in your heart
I want to feel your warmth
Even for a few soft burns
What pages have you torn,
Burned,
And scraped
Your candle
I yearn for wax
What was it that freed you?
When life had you trapped
While out the window
Gazing
You longed to soar
And speak your turn

Wings spread
Vodka burns
So much more than
A single Swallow
I think reclined
Back on obsidian chairs
The young pale eyes
Gazing unaware
How his skin reflected
many a stare
Hidden from the sun's affair
He'd watch the stage
As the actors' dance
Their voices combined in some
Harmonious rave
And all that was there
The glint of gold,
Decay
He watched the sparkle
The glam
The harking of contenders
Dawning masks
For a grand display
While she grew taller
Made many a penny
Squallier
A loving brother
Dare not ponder
The mask upon his face
Displayed
The dancers indulged

A soiree
My phantom watching
A masquerade
As he grew taller
In silver moonlight
Wandered
Seeking within whispering woods
Amongst devils
Distant figure's hoods
His own parade,
Wondering
what sort of twisted golem
Hell displayed
Wandering out of a shadow
Squawking
"Paradise!"
Not so sober before the crap
Rolling a pair of dice
A boring game
of odds and fate

Old Guitar

Nothing makes me smile more
Than plucking the strings
Of my acoustic
Counterpart
A long day winds down
Drags me thin
Had put me in a place
Where my head spins
I take it in stride
Kiss goodbye
The day old demise
When I strum a melody
That makes my spirit rise
The twang and how I sang
On late nights
With a bottle not far
All faded
Behind the slide
Of my fingers across
My old guitar
The golden strings
And how they sing
I'd never be able to part
Even when it sounds like shit
Ill strum along
The beat of the heart
Singing of hope
Beyond empty pain
Beautiful as

Chimes in the rain
There's little more soothing
Than the strum
Of my old guitar
I need something to believe
Something to hold
But it's 3 a.m.

I'm laying in bed
Embracing the cold

From the moment I learned to speak
I was told
"Now listen."
But that was bullshit,
To begin with
Now whether I be
In a marching crowd
Or leaning back in my yard
Underneath Summer clouds
I'll listen while the cicadas sing
And my friends beautiful and distant
Are laughing.
Gathered around
Dancing
Either giggling in locked cars
Or laying on a dock
Beneath the northern stars
I'll listen
Hear them
Without the orders to follow
A group who wanted
Another voice
To join in
Their complacent prattle
Or to chitter and tattle over
Disagreement
No,
I will be silent
And smile
Because the moment they spoke
I didn't bother

To stop and listen

If I could remove
One thing
I'd take the flame
Throw it away
From this calcium frame
Id stamp the ground
And feel more proud
Of the burn scars
Craved
If I could say
Just one thing
I'd tell you of
The Shame
I hate myself
For all the anger
inside me
The transparent rage
Starring
Into a mirror
I see
Our faces
Are the same

I don't care about the nights
My sister tucked me in
While I was lulled
By your shouting

I care I came home
My mother was crying
While my sister held her hand
"Your father is gone"

I don't care about why you left
I learned it's easier to forget
Learning to forgive you
Was one of my hardest tests

And Still I'll never forget
The emptiness
The regret
The anger that grew
In my chest

My only care is
You do yours
And I'll do my best
To learn to love
Myself

The greatest test yet

It came so fast
Like a stray wind
On an ill taken voyage
A tidal charge
I remember looking out at the ocean
While my mother and sister sighed
I found only the horizon
Captivated my eyes
What lies beyond there?
And what's the difference from here?
Why do they find comfort?
In something I found fear.
What are fears?
What are desires?
I look in the mirror
And whisper
'You look so tired'
Maybe that's the way it goes
Like how the river
Can bend and flow
Or be shapely as midnight tears
Drowning in your heart's absence
Of warmth

    I don't want to go
    I find it harder to stay
    The face in the mirror
    I don't recognize today
    Staring into yours,
    Deep as the ocean wide
    Drowning behind my own eyes

These days are so strange
The brisk cool wind
That tickles my neck
The shady sky
Painted with rolling greys
Mellow sunlight
That does not warm
Yet within it
A calm,
Reflects.
I enjoy these days
Where silence is best
Met only with
The soft hum of music,
In another room
While I rest
On my grandfather's couch
Watching the breeze
Brushing the hair of Pines'
Eternal green
The sky always seemed
A painting to me
Something I couldn't shake
The first-time I'd seen
It filled me with a longing
To stand on cloudy peaks
But pressed against these cushions
I smile
Rather not to speak
In that moment
I'm floating above

That distant peak

There is nothing but silence and breeze
Gently billowing,
Green leaves.
Their white sleeves
Wrapped like swaddled newborns
In darkened coats,
Eyes fallen like sands
Through final moments
Of sharply curving glass
That first clink
So long forgotten

Brothers
Sat at bars stools
Spinning tales of battles
Prevailed
Together they laugh
Red faced
Styled by the seas
Sailed

Moor the ship
And let us return
To simpler times
Where life was loved
Underneath
The ever blue sky
Souls fine
As aged wines
Sipped beside the crowded street
where lovers met

To dine

Once the final breath
Is passed
eyes to flutter closed
At last
We share one last laugh
The dollar slides
Across carven wood
to split the cask

Not to ask
Was each action
As perfect as the last
Instead
We refine our spirits
that each was as meaningful
As the last

I reached out once
And received no ends
My words fell upon silence
Chilling
As the early morning clear
Maybe a year
Or close enough
Id taken my things
But their words and memories
Still built up
A tower coated in sweat
My hands slick
Clutching my head
Being eaten from the inside out
That parasite,
Regret
I reached out
Finding no railing
No overwhelming confidence
Or closure prevailing
Merely a haunt
My gaze turned to
The passing of ghosts
White tooth smiles became
Yellowed
I yoked myself
From the murky waters
In unwashed clothes
And half cashed ash
Bobbing for sympathy
Red delicious and ambrosia

Sweet nectar that is shame
Siccing flies upon
Caramel coated memories
I Thought detained
Only I see
The peels of my skin
Curl and memory
Stains more
Than chalk on garage floors
Where ashes lay
Carefully tapped
A concussive smack
Across the sheen of
Old wooden plane
The ashes and freshly cut apples
My tongue tastes no sweeter
From nicotine and
Butane lighters
Live and let memories die,
In the end
All those pretty crystals
Tasted the same,

Now my hand
Remain steady
My sinuses clear
Reaching no longer
For soon
I will taste apples again

Three young men
Dragons in their pockets
Blackened out sockets
Dreams fresher than cut
Grass
Spoken word and turned phrase
To hidden idols
Giving praise
Not coated by gold
But the accomplishment pulled
From trailers and a back water
Living space
Our own paces
Fading in sand
By the Missouri
Sorting through damp papers
Ink running down
Their changing faces
Darkened eyes
Harder sighs
The last call
Crescent ball
spinning over the floor
None of my old lovers' dance
To these beats anymore
I took my tracks
what little posted notes
Tacked
To the cork board
Crack another can
While the musician

Packed up the van
I stood on the roadside
With a bottle in my hand
Wondering will I learn to sing
Like those Bards again

I took time away
Left without words
Not out of animosity
I'd try and claim
But jealousy
Perhaps these are two shades
All but
Tasting the same
They who smile
Carrying their burdens away
While my eyes drifted further down
My efforts
We're circling a drain
If I'd stayed
There's no telling how I'd fair
My fears and anger were growing
And my purpose here
Was no longer clear
Playing games
Uninviting to change
My hands trying to take hold
When I had already lost the reins
So deep within silence
My will withered
Nothing felt real
Every breath stolen
Choking on the splinters
My fingers,
To bite and peel
Seeking fortune from others
Who long slaved,

For Their music
Swallowing myself
I carried on
I still carry on
Looking for the melody
I've lost

My life no longer filled
With song

Sometimes I feel them
My crumpled wings
They spread

For a moment

I feel
As though
I am
Not quite
Dead

Eyes can speak
You can witness in them
The stories untold
Memories kept from aging
Storms to behold
That burning chest
Tightly holds
Unable to let go
They who care not
Which path they take
Or what destiny unfolds
Hold them close
Unforgotten loves,
The memories you chose
Let them be the guiding post
Lamps
In the darkest rooms
We find their light
Flicks the spark that whispers
Have hope
For those who love hardest
That choke on words they wished
Written
With no ink
Their blood and tears
The pages soak
In them you'll find
"I love you"
Are the most beautiful words
Ever spoke

I wish I could pass all my time with you
To bask in the warmth of a summer's
Delight
I'd feel your grace caressing my skin
And like so many nights alone
For you
I would sing
But I have no foundations
I'm not all I seem
I wish I could be as I appear
Like vapors
I'm bound to disappear
I wander the woods
Just to keep my mind clear
While you dance between twilights
Without fear
I've spent too long staring into mirrors
I'm afraid of what
I can't see clear
What a dream
To dance with you in my arms
But I've been a fool
Can't play any new part
For as long as I can bask in your light
I'll withstand to be in your heart
For as long as you'll have me near
I'll keep watching
Headlights to a deer
If I wander to close
They'll bury me in the warmth
Of a midsummer's day

With a smile
I'll be fond of that lost grace
That which washed away fear
Don't shed tears for me my dear
I'll always be smiling
The rest of your years

Love in the present
You are not your past
The future is unwritten
And there are still new paths
Travel with yourself
As if walking with your friends
Expose your heart to forgiveness
For the happiness you upend
Learn to laugh and love
And to feel the beating heart
When frustration comes
Don't tear up that page
There's so much more to you
Than you see
Understand the truth behind
My words

You are always free

When I turned to look away
I heard a boy call my name
Looking back I saw him there
To me he looked so afraid
His joints profound
His eyes casting away
What little light left in them
Began to fade
Stammering I tried to ask
"What's wrong?"
He replied
'Nothing. I'm okay.'
And I still couldn't look away
His clothes were heavy
Despite the summer heat
The hair on his head
Matted down a greasy shroud
He hasn't showered in days
When I tried to step forward
He quickly stepped away
'Don't come back!'
It had been a while
But I recognized his face
Struggling with a small smile
He asked
"Do you regret me?"
"Don't worry kid. It'll take a little time."
I turned away.
"But you'll be better than just okay!"

I heard him giggle

As he began to fade
I swear I'll never forget
The smile he finally gave

What Is This Haunting Feeling?

What is this haunting feeling
Following me like a bad dream
Creeping its way,
In strange particular ways
Even after I've had a good day
Am I not meant to be happy?
Am I not allowed to sleep easy?
Must each night stretch longer,
Until my mind tears at its seams?
What can I say to understand?
What can I write here?
Whatever stains these pages
Be it blood or tears?
Or a burning hatred that sears my throat
As I scream and try to write another note or line!
What sort of tunnel has become of my mind!
The further I try and seek
Only darker apparitions appear
With the same stupid grin
I wear
Myself out
And take to the floor
Nothing less
Nothing more
I feel as though I was meant for more
Something other than late nights
And stifled lip morns
What else is there
What am I searching for

A will or a reason
With each changing season
I feel myself
Struggle less and sob more
I'm carefree yes but I still wish
I could care less
And be undisturbed by the frantic
Obsession
To blame myself
For my own depression

Some days are rough
You're put to the test
Somedays you want to quit
Laying in bed
Stinking from sweat
So stressed
But if anyone asked
You'd profess
"I'm good. How are you?"
Some Days
It's just easier to deflect
And as much as you'd like to rest
That pounding in your chest
The weight on your back
This beast we call stress
You haven't been drowned yet
Though we are strange
Maybe deranged
Trains of thought off the rails
It's out of radio range
I'll bet
Like anyone else you want to say
It's not over.
I'm not done!
I want to be free!
So be free and run
But if you do
Wherever you are
Whether laying in bed
Or sitting alone in the car
You my friend

Keep these words
Have heart!

Rest now and wake later
Listen to the gentle patter
The rain coming down around midnight
Just before you lay your head
The many chilled pillows
Two comforters and a quilt
Wrapping your body
Leaving an exposed head
You take deep breaths
Sigh each away
For as long as you lay there
Sleep might not come your way
Rest now and wake later
Envelope yourself in your own warmth
The radiator is broken
But you didn't mind
Even in the dead of winter
You enjoy a cool breeze sometimes
Rest now wake later
Alone in a creaking house
Your family doesn't really knock
But you recognize the old wooden door
By the sound of its closing
It resounds and shakes the house
The creeping footsteps
Muffled whispers
You recognize your sister's voice
You recognize the boy of choice
Resting now and waking later
Warmed by yourself and not the radiator
The shallow light creeps through red curtains

It's bright out
But the hour?
You're more or less uncertain
Early afternoon
Later in the morning
The wind brushes against the house
A familiar hollow moaning
As if it were abandoned
You it's final tenant
The shade that wanders these halls
Unforgiving
It drags along like unpacked luggage
Stuffed in the corner left unopened
And dusty
The bathroom littered by makeup,
Accessories
A brush and razor
I keep kept in the same place
The dry carve of cold metal on pale skin
You don't need a head start
Or as many cosmetics
A few bracelets on your arm
With a necklace
In the afternoon your days begins
Not to go downstairs
But shuffle behind a thin door
Resting at the screen on top stacked books
A few small towers that dress a bedroom floor
No message or texts
Maybe a single call to collect
The brightness of a screen

An unblinking reflection
There you'll rest and wake later
Finding it colder to go outside
The world that rests here
Waking later

Vices and virtues
Cripple by my vices
Obsessed with your image
Unseen angels, A vision of virtue
Floating above these dank cellar walls

Yet in the early morning
Stirs your slender figure to rise
Ears filled with songs
And the glare of oceans eyes
Cracked to the pursued lips
Mumbling of the absurd and dawn

If forgotten how quickly between sleep
My memory slips of what was said
Not that I meant to be heard
You'd lay there for hours picking at scabs
eyes that which betray any concern
Just another upturned stone
The unseen moistened earth
Is never brought to mind,
Of worms

And how, Lets speak,
Of vices I'm stained
My hands clutch paper notes
You never learn to read
What a pain it must be
For us to talk so often
Yet hardly ever speak

What virtue lies in my silence
Of the vices you're unsure
And opaque cylinders stir no life
From white spore caps spurred

Two sometimes makes no one
Of concern?
Tell me how absurd
To delve into your fantasies
Yet the waters of the sink are undisturbed
The mirror reflection
Makes my own eyes blur
And at the last drop of absinthe
A noise finally made of her

She grinned and spilled over
My wretched contents
Rising through my lungs
To make them burn

All I ever was
In trying to be held within her
Trying to grow a garden
Inside a dank cistern

My brother who watched by my side
Giving a strong hand against tired back
Alone within the exhausted sighs
And empty gaze of sunken eyes

Telling me not of truths
Or a reassuring compromise
Between ours
Bonds thicker than paint
I'm sure within your remarks
Come no lies

Silently sat beside me as I lowered
Much into a digging fanatical craze
My nails whittled down
My muscles ache
Passing affectionately
A lit cigarette in an open grave

You'd take not shovels and hoes
Not descend in my place
Your fixed grin behind
The sullen gaze that lacked
Homely grace
In the face of that
Those hideous moments
Your words were better paths
Led to the salvations that followed

Of this and that
Of our presents and pasts

The dark lying scoundrels
Who now lay upon a rack
Their backs displayed
With no marked names
Tied sticks with brittle bones
And notes held down by paper weights

I'll miss them
Our idle conversations
Clever turns of phrase
The laughter shared over coffee
Even in moments without pace
You'd turn my head to the sun
Shown through transfixed glass
Averted,
My old reluctance to praise

Take me now from this sunken ground
The head's final resting place
And gift me with vigor
So I may return
Beneath the faded auburn sky
I'll find you resting on the hillside
With a pair of cancer sticks unburned

Well talk of this and that
For a moment
A single lasting moment
The favor I'll return
Tell you of all the world's mysteries
Of all I've learned

I wanted to create something beautiful
Something worth talking about
A floating dream that drifted
While I was growing apart
A deserted garden
Or an abandoned amusement park
Cobblestone paths disappearing
Under tenacious weeds
Copper colored railings rusted
Choked by the vines of the overgrowth
When the sun finally set
The silhouettes were erased
A candle burns solemnly
In a darker embrace
Staring into its quiet ballet
You begin to ask
'Whose face is that gazing back?'
A memory maybe
Or the very thing you lost
A warmth leaving the vigorous body
A corpse replaced
I wanted to create something beautiful
Out of that darkened place
Unable to recognize what parts of me
Are original
And the ones I've replaced

Long late night cruises
Eyes misty in a rising sun's haze
Red strings running through us
Disguised as veins
Forever entwined in fate
Now only a drifting memory remains
Monarchs spread wings
After their change
Looking into her stare then
I knew
Like them I had to change
Pleading with myself
I could feel blood boiling in my veins
Disguising my fear behind excuses
Reasons I was running late
I'll never know if she would have felt the same
What I didn't understand
Was how hard it is
For metamorphosis to begin
After leaving that car
I never felt whole again

You will find peace
Maybe not today
Maybe not tomorrow
But never lie to believe
You'll always be incomplete

You will find peace
There is an end to sorrow
In small moments of bliss
Shared laughing fits
The memories stirred into coffee
To reminisce

You will find peace
I promise this
In the whirlwinds that may follow
The struggles starved until tomorrow
Whisper this

I will find peace
There is end to rain
I will love myself
And forgive my pain
I will become peace
And be kinder to my needs
Unafraid to hold my care
Above others wants and needs
You are peace
Take it day by day
Week by week
And when you feel weak

Come back to the here and say

I will find my peace

I laughed this morning
with tears in my eyes
Laying back on my bed
Letting the laughter spread
Dove into memory and the stranger things I've
said
I wondered how it became so natural
To fall asleep with dread
I'd sit in front of a brightened screen
Tapping my restless leg
Pondering dreams
Wandering back into taverns
Where the raven haired girl sings
My eyes yellowed by the things
Better left unseen
Drunk until the morning's rise
To brush my missing teeth
I lay against my bed and found
Eyes glistening
Id not crossed the river
Yet the raft around me
Began disassembling

When the flames in young souls
Cease their burning
The folds of their youth's ingenuity
Smooth their crease
From the forthcoming dreams,
No boldness
But reclined sighs
In chairs that creak.
Burdened by the days
Of ceaseless deceit
That life become shrugged,
Unloved,
Is any more complete than those
Who in late night's evocative whispers
Come creeping
Spilling,
Not vials of nightshade,
But glasses
Full of their spirit's tears
Squeezed out from grapes
Contorting,
Their hopes and wonders
Were simply inventions
Born of youthful yearnings
To chase and smolder
Desires of
Glistening rings and chandeliers
Courting eyes
Discerning studies
Of all that glitters
Only to find their cups

Not filled with gold
But the bitter taste of barely
Rolling down a closing throat
Coated in scents of mold
Finding home
In your sheets
If it hurts too much
To stand
Get off your feet
If it's more comforting
Just sleep

There's a hole in my door
My grandpa asked
"Where did that come from?"
"Must have been there before."
It was three years ago
A sunless summer day
I was just a kid
Who didn't want to play
Any of the games
my tenants played
The father came over
But I didn't hear any bells
That solemn Sunday
In the yard all I saw
Were lights
Stifled breaths
Some prying eyes
Curious of why the sheriff
Dressed like a preacher
Still carried a strap
The father told me how lucky
I am to never feel
The same clap
Of his father's wrath
"Praise my restraint!"
The father told me
As he was leaving
My thoughts entirely
That was the day of the fire
After that I saw
God I'd never seen anything brighter

Flames swallowed
My grandpas house
Drinking a whole bottle
Was all I thought about
Wash away under sheets
Not rain
Instead a tornado
Sent books, paper,
And a chair
Against the door
Leaving a small hole
Where a boy
Was left lying
Never balanced
The same as before
As a slammed door

Gate
Beneath the sunless sky
Where I lay
Gazing but not seeing
Open eyes
Shut like shutters
Tied with golden chains
The moon shone a stone path
Guiding my way

Gate
Seek the moonless night
Going out in ripples of black water
Rolling around my waist
Weighed down by word and phrase
Gemstones sewn to a crown
Floating in the wake

Paragate
Hearing no voice
My fingers like knots
Cradling the floating petals
Beyond where the tide
Meets the sky
No lightning flickers
Nor stars dance
Behind tired eyes

Parasamgate
And my strangled woes
Held in fetters

Muscles ache over stroked letters
Now lying beneath
The sunless sky

Bodhi Svaha

I've got the wild stuck in my head
My hands are growing heavy
My eyes shot red
And in the evening
I speak with the dead
They tell me
They are waiting
At the water's edge
As I gazed into the blackened depths
I hoist my sails
Turning to the north
Some fool without a map
Set with sails of poor choice
I'll drink to the peace of my friends
Of course
But should they ask where I went
I hope they are convinced
I am dead
Where I am going
Is not for them
Truly the voyager is left un-condemned
But the mad wanderer
with bottle in his hand
Will laugh of his miserable spirit
With the rest of the damned

I hope you find the strength
To say
This is not okay
And walk away
The burden you shoulder
Is heavy
But the river
Must be forged
Even if it carries down stream
A little ways
There is strength in you
Growing day by day
I hope you find your peace
In pens and paper
Paints or clay
Nothing is more beautiful
Than your unwavering soul
Nothing is more inspiring
Than you rising
Every new day

I'm getting better
Fighting a little harder
Striding a little farther
What's a sculpture,
Without its carvings?

On a cloudy day
I saw my shadow
Knowing the light shines on me
Wherever I'll go

Regrets left in midnight texts
Stressed over my stumbling steps
I reached out with fingers
Tap dancing

It's easier for me to dance after a few drinks

My confession left the early morning
With a sick sense of self-serving threats
Empty stomach,
Full of thought
Chased liquor
Down a wet chin

A burry stare
A wryly grin
My skin slick
Whirlpools churns within
All about some girl
Fancy a chance
To never begin

Taste out the amber glass,
And let your
Head spin
The room like a carousel
The Cage
I've locked myself in

My room is stacked with pages written
While I'm consumed by the unwritten
Prints lost to another night of swallowing
Bourbon out my grandfather's kitchen
The vodka ran dry
Down with choked tears
Regret reared its ugly head to
Grave robbing all those emotions
I thought were better left
To sneer and jeer at
My own pain

Played out under tap dancing fingers
To a girl a thousand miles away
Now in the mornings embrace
I feel like my insides are twisted vines
And every thought of her is taken
With a swig of vodka
To chasers and runaways

Weeds sprouted
Where petals ought to be
Digging deep
A fear of uncertainty
Would I ever be the same?
After running this long
My feet bled
Against the concrete
My fears clawing and
Crawling beneath
It bleeds as I try
To hold my core
The doors are gone
What's more?
They've broken from their hinges
Forced open
Letting through remorse

I tried to move on
Keep my head down
No casting lights
Could cast the shadows out
And still in my forced imprisonment
I felt my voice give it all
To scream!
And I swatted
At the hands held out!
I fought for awhile
I dove into the bottle
Throttled it
Like my own neck
Make some form of this
Shapeless motto
I'd be better off carrying on alone
My choices led me down this path
To a road
I used to walk so well
Now it has become hollow
The visage of a ghost
Will I ever hold someone again
Or face this world on my own

Being a campfire
To warm others
Only leaves you burned
When the fire finally dies
They'll move on at sunrise
Leaving just your ashes
Gray as
Empty goodbyes

Just because you've bled beside them
Doesn't mean you'll always fight the same
battles
People heal in different ways.
Though the scars remain
Their shapes are never
Quite the same

How quickly my love of golden fields
Turned sour
Their grains yellow
Rotted beneath an acid rain
The wild grasses
Of rolling plains
Became weeds
Unfamiliar
Broken glass
Betrayed the vision
Of a younger face
My hands shook
Cut palms and rust
Become an old familiar taste
Hands tracing sullen sockets
Where hoped drained down
Black velvet ballads
Of betters loves and
Evergreen wakes
Warmer beds undisturbed
Before dawning
Another bowl and bat
Another hit to take away the ennui
Id suffocate

Today a new dawn greets me
Humbled by that haze
The days I'd stare
Into the golden plains
Free and wild for a time
Mere child's play
Unafraid of the wind or storms
Until my hands missed the warmth
My tired eyes watching the dust float
Between her rays
I've learned to sculpt a new spirit
From stone
Corroded by acid rain

I can't stay here!
Where the sky doesn't move
Locked behind the thin frame
Of a cluttered gray bedroom

I can't stay here!
Where the voices loom
And my eyes see no light
Behind the curtains
Until the dust dances
Between the invasive
Beams of noon

I can't stay here!
My spirit no longer stirs
Nothing fills my chest
I'm so obsessed with longing it hurts
My stomach aches
Sleepless nights
leave my eyes salted
How they burn

I can't stay here!
With the thought of being
A caged bird
My wings folded
Molting across wire floors
I sulk afraid
To see them spread
To try and fly again
Without being a burden

I'm sorry you can't stay
To say another word
This place has consumed every hope
For what you've yearned
Soon you'll be,
little more than bones
And scribbled words
Forgotten like a stain
Left on pages no longer read
No longer turned
After sacrificing so much
You've forgotten to take
What's yours
The undeniable right
To hold something close
You've given enough
Your eyes have become
So heavy
Hands held by your lover
Feel coarse
They don't flinch
They don't turn away
It's love after all
Why are you so afraid?
Maybe they'll be different
You feel so many different things these days
Still I know that look
Take it step by step
Love doesn't come easy
Or so they say
After you've turned them all away

It'll be a long road
And in the dark our fears
Find romance with anxiety
Together they play
Turn yourself towards them
Hold them close and whisper
I'd rather fight to love,
Than throw my heart away

Love what you will
Keep it close
Let those who can weather
Find their own coasts
Between the lines of this universe
And each other's
To sisters and brothers
Who shoulder,
One another
Let them transverse
This terrible curse
Of pain and wonder
Eyes to plunder
Plucked jewels
From the sky
And heart-felt goodbyes
We'll wander towards,
New shores
Together

A warped perception
That pushed me to the edge
Maybe a symptom of depression
All my attentions
Shrouded under
"Good intent"
Makes no difference
When you're staring
Off a cliff
Knowing this is it
Where the road ends
You wonder if you're lost
You start to make maps and charts
Calculate the chaos
Lurking in your heart
What exactly
Was the cost?
For a few moments of bliss
Hard to resist the temptation
Of being rid
Of 'this'
All the loneliness
And all that rage
Clawing at your own skin
Like it's a cage
Starring in the reflection of a glass pipe
Or downing someone else's prescription
Just to feel right
It isn't
That's the truth behind the mask
The anger behind each gritted tooth

And split lip you bite
Tearing yourself apart with
Consumption
Inst something id prescribe
But what's conveyed from
A few short rhymes
Back then I was different
And it feels
Like I've lived two lives
Arrived at another roads end
Another cliff dive
This wasn't the last time
I've fallen
It won't be the last time
I've died
But each one I've learned
To be a little more kind
No one else is going to make me feel
Not an empty bottle or pills to grind
Will give back the peace of mind
I sold
For a few hours of being high
On these pages
I'll recount the pain
Even if i have to scream
Until my throat bleeds
A thousand more times
Even if no one is listening
It's not for sympathy or pleasure
I beat out my lifeline
It's to pull myself

Back to shore
So Isle be
of a more tranquil mind

Consumption I've known
Tuberculosis of the soul
To fill up pills and bottles
Warm drunkenness
That washes
Clean of my soul
Wandering under a gaze
I don't feel I belong
And still I'm drawn
To the ones unique
Together
In a welcoming call home
Bright in their grins
Their fleeting holds
On words and phrase.
Memories of times
With laughter we rolled
Down empty streets
Stood proud on corners
To meet-
Death,
Was never the price of the toll
But a price of life
And when the hour grows late
And I'm left with hands alone
Or arms which I've held
I shiver
To the whisper's chills
The winds
That make sails full
Come home out of the cold

My love
Stories are yet unspoken
Lives yet to unfold
With their broken voices
Herald me with the bold
Who thrust their guts
Into dying hearths and
Empty hearts
Yearning for something more
The icy winds and the cries
Of distant church bells
Priests to mutter
This story so young
And already older
Than we've known
Remember it fondly
For we must all pay the toll
Of life lived
And the hands we hold
The adventures better
Remembered
When unasked for

Lights inside my chest
But are they lamps,
Or balls of fire,
A multicolored flame
Burning black, grey,
White, red, and orange
All them the same
Burning on against
Pounding rain
Quick to spark
Dying in plainness
How could I explain this?
But through art
I'm unbound by chains
Chasing yellow streetlamps
Embers of exhaled
Nicotine
That stains my breath
When will this rotting die
My soul colorful
Pulsing beneath my skin
Turned cold
Express your burns
"Undying flame"
Whispered of my nameless
Soul

People I love become sad
From my words and my phrase
These bled out rhymes
Coating a wrinkled page
Two mares tied
By red strings
Pulling me in their ways
One towards prosperity
The other
Less than sublime
Each one pulls at my limbs
Running out of time
Time.
Time....
For a change
While my thoughts
Circle clocks
Hours and seconds
Spinning down the drain
My feet stained by mud and twigs
This skin
Constricts like a reptile
Ill slink between
Stones and grass
Where you're sitting
Whispering of what could be
Or isn't quite what
It truly is
Illusions made in smoke
Where unbridled emotions
Are choked

Numbness be stoked within
Fire
No longer burning
Desires
For which this flesh
No longer yearns
Let me become like god
In the eyes of the world
Become
"Known"
Eyes cold
As cobble pathways'
Stone

What it is to
The many doors
Winding staircases
How they open with wonder
Before the stars reflected
In a lover's eyes before setting suns
Spilling stories
Three sheets to the wind
Of my friend
Who plays with the fire
In his hands
Rumblings and ramblings
Of truths
To withstand
Tests of time
Familiar faces
What's bent in our minds
Stood in far out places
Trace the constellations to find
Where you are
Guiding arts spoken
In midnight's
Cruising cars
Sparks between eyes
Tender kiss of life
Brutal is the changing wind
Where does my story end?
Where did I try to begin?
Listen…

All I am
Are stories
Memories melted across
A dimly lit screen
Dusted pages of books
Tearing at their seams
Words that fall haunting
From chapped lips
And soothsayers
Be my brethren
On torrid storm,
Challenged,
Merchant ships
Sailed through nights
Into windy hills
Numb these aches with vodka
And a side of soda swilled

One day
All I'll be
Is a memory
Stories left lingering hearts
Of those who witnessed me
And on the nights
Where winds howl and roll
Shaking the windows to beckon
The winters cold
My voice will come drifting across
The snowy shore
A vision of a shadow
Leaving a trail alone

They might turn briefly
Under yellow streetlamps
As if I'd just passed
For a moment
The embers
Come to live with them again
I wonder what stories they'll
Remember
My loving ends

Take these words
Mutilate me
Exhaustion
Take these wings
Crucified
Fears
Run rampant in my heart
Passions
Trample me
Let my spirit roam
Set this house on fire!
Burn these papers!
Their warmth
Free me

This time
I don't feel real
Like I'm just dust
Without purpose
My reality
My identity
Is only electricity
Firing signals in a shell
In those moments
I can't describe fear
I ask questions
To quantify so many
Unanswered thoughts
A list miles long
I wonder if I can cut this cyst
Take a blade to my skin
Carve some new constellations
What maps might they bring
New horizons
The end to long nights
Or will I only ride further
Into the mists
I desperately fight
Will I be free of my guilt?
Of the slights and aggression
I produced
After sleeping with Erebus
Might we create some
Divine truth
Or will there be no more
Me

Just dirty rags
Once my form, reduced
Dust traveling out
From a toppled vase
My words and worries
Burnt up
My incessant need to live
Hurried
Gone in a breath
Without trace
The constellations might remain
Crowns shimmering
Above the sea
Reflecting across
Calm waves
Guiding others
To something familiar
Or something entirely new
I'll reach with my last strength
To ask
Do all wanderers
Feel so out of place?

The brief silence
Embrace me
All that provokes me
Desire
Leave me
What yet possesses
Rage
Release me
What I long to hold
Compassion
Take me

Hallucinating

They say the soul exists
Within the heart
So I sold mine for a bottle and a carton of sticks
Left behind the only part of me
That persists
To be content with all of
"This"
Sadness and anger
The feeling I'm my own stranger
I'll wager
I never truly knew myself
Like my father
How my mother
Holds her distance
Persistence was a sure way to lose me
And the booze became
The only thing I truly felt
Sacred
No gods come down
For representation
No flags lay claim
I'm not into self-degradation
I'm just stuck here on the porch
Taking drags
Wondering what it's like to love
Because it's something
I've never had
I'm mad contemplating
Thinking about my own

Issues identification
These feelings that only flow
When I'm left with disturbed
Just another mental patient
Highly irregular
My only love
Hallucinating
And tonight
I'm contemplating
A life well lived is
Negatives and positives
But where's the line draw
Between
what's good
What's made to be regulated
How many more nights
Will I sit here
Anticipating
My own end
Or the ends by
Which I'm to guide the ends
Of God's given
Dividends
Does God see the end?
Or is he just
Hallucinating
Does he think in circles?
Or deep contemplation
Am I really the cause
Or am I just
Hallucinating

The pit that digs deep down in my gut
Fantasies of what is and what wills
Rising bile
Thick like sludge
Keeping the anxiety
Held in my blood
Pumping first to my heart
Then into my brain
Where the rest goes is what's often
Left to fade away
Behind the fogged misty windows
And panes
Shrouded beneath the droplets
Sacred palms
Hide my eyes with shade
And well-off partners
Sharing drinks
Tell me exactly
The last time
Someone whispered your name
I'll tell you mine
But you'll only speak
From time to time
Gently tapping glass
Serpent fingers
Coil,
This ring of mine
Comprised of silver
Compose me a simpler
Medium
To sway this confusion

And drain away
the empty attempts to speak
Sweeter things to her
And wash away this bile
Growing
Where choice wasn't heard
Behind the way
The Tarot turns

To live as if
You're always asleep
Perhaps in that way
We'll always be
In our dreams
The things once lost
Hope filled imagination
Regained
Free of harmful thoughts
Only the gentle
Rise and fall
Of peaceful exasperation
What joy could be found
What sort of amalgamations
We might create
Profound
Full of lucid thought
Held so close
Without worry
Never to be released
Never to fade
To live
As if we are sleeping
Gentle to carry on
Lost in our dreams
Across
Forever fluorescent stains
In a prison of my own making
Sweat stained nightmares
Caught my breath between
Paralysis dreams

And all the voices sinking deep
Between
What no longer seems
Just simple nights of sleep
Whether to be caught in mornings
Reluctant urgencies
Or fall between
My anxious sheets

Blue pills and Nyquil
Won't make my mind
Clean
With eyes wandering from the corner
Where the fanged hounds creep
Watching
Draped in midnight
His poacher not far
From underneath
My frame does creak and creak
Hours disappearing
Like burning white sheets
Of paper where my eyes left
Darkened streaks
To try and record these visions
Hoarded deep
Behind violet eyelids
The feeling I'm not alone
Whenever I go to sleep

Is this how I'll remain
A link in a chain
Is it the depression that speaks
My inner monologue
So meek?
Let the serpents sing and gallows sway
I can't sleep
Nothing seems to change
The bleak mosaic
That stares to the window
Saying I'm going to die
In the same cage
Locked up by thoughts
When the venom invades
I won't eat
I'll just lay
I won't speak
Ill complain
Every moment
Passing grains of salt
And say
"Fucking bullshit!"
All the same
Trapped inside my name
Trapped inside a skin
Better left hanging in the corner
Than put on display
Freak they'll claim
'Menace' and 'Rage'
These are my names
But rest doesn't remain

When the visions begin to lay
Their product
In a locked room
Scribbling in notebooks
Black pens and body pins
Mark down all the words in blood
Because I can't find the best verse to say
Five simple words

I live in a cage

Those moments
Sips of coffee
Bad jokes
Times spent
Laughing over
Stupid jokes
Hold onto them
Hold close
Your memories
Keep them safe
Wipe away the dust
When you can't escape
The torrent of worry
The nagging
Anxious
Hurry!
Fall back on compassion
Love
Behind blurry eyes
It's there
You felt it
You touched it
A candle's flame
Warm
Behind those old doors
Passion was formed
Take hold of my hands
Feel their warmth
I'm here with you
Wherever you go
My sister

My brother
I love our memories
Let them flow

How vividly we retreat into ourselves
Pouring out our thoughts and passions
Like jugs of water
To fervent springs
Drawing near sprites
Never have I tasted waters
So sincere
Than watching her hands
Glide across the canvas
To drink her own wellspring
The dripping tears of paint
Excited fears that illuminate
All she shed
Grasped
Afraid to speak too loudly
Of all she held dear
Might soon sink beneath
Misunderstandings and uncertainty
Drawing vacant eyes and half finished sketches
Near completion and all the more
Invoking for what was still lurking
Behind her
Pushed
Dark brown hair behind her ears
Fingers blessed by the paints
Things we can't say
Retain
Or speak plain
Fears holden to me
Touching such beautiful colors
My stains might just as easily

Take theses colors and smear
So vividly
I'll retreat back into my own
Thoughts and fears
Never saying a word
How dark my art would remain?
On my own easel
Until id witnessed
All the beauty in her paints
Have I ever tasted water,
So clear?

I've known plenty of souls
Some who still wander
Distant plains
Some who have reclined
Into heartfelt moments
And remain
The last words spoken
My memory of them unchanged
I've known many souls
Who charge towards bright days
Their hearts full
As the wings of predatory birds
Still their spirits are soaring
Like the distant
Thousand-mile journey
Planes
All have come settled or unsettled
And though the visions of their features
Are full of luster
None for long seem to remain

Who am I too judge?
What should go or stay
We've got one journey
That's life
As much as we'd like to claim
"Remember the last time we met?"
"Man, I'm still the same."
I've known many people
Changing day by day
Their hearts righteous

Some who surrendered
Let themselves lay and still
To exhume theme
You'd find their forms
Decayed
Swaying between the lines and roads
The places we'd claim as homes
Souls floating between
The fettered lanes
Lovers and fighters
The proud and the lame
I've known many people
Along my path
Only a few ever remain
Somehow, I still hold them close
Hoping and waiting
For the day well share a drink
And tell our stories
Again

Two trees standing before me
One dead
Where the bird houses still sway
The other teeming with life
So fervent with life
That undergrowth chokes beneath
All things seem to be connected
In the arms of a raging storm
And all I wonder is
If I'm more one than the other
A weed or shelter
Dead or born
Or am I
Caught in the cycle?

Branches yet to reach
Ready to soar

Is this part of your works?
The tightened strings
Hooks tearing open my throat
Slack jawed angels
Who watch the world
Yearn for things desired
Unprovoked
To good news or bad
We ponder
Unseen
Unheard of
Or are you tying my noose?
If all things be tied and bound
To happen within
The determined breaths
We take
These stones
Dragging behind me
Cast them into
A burning sea
Let me inhale the sulfur
And become grotesque
Your words and chirps
Make of me
Black swan swings
Will blot the sun
Good men will fall
To the rising tide
Swallowing
What little things we seek
Then will you leave me be

Fate?

Or both shall we fall
Like stars
Burning so brilliantly
Til only silence remains
To keep corpses
Smelling sweet
To devour ourselves
Souls to keep

The comets that crash against jade waves
Burning stars,
Slipping out of gaze
Wild eyes
Lay witness to the sea
Storms,
To guide my way
The blindness of my soul
Screams to let loose
The lucid doors
Create these distant worlds
And rattle
The binding cage
Set me free
As the song filled sea
Calming is the sting of her breeze
Setting free
these thoughts
Binding me
into causes
lost
Held closely
Until at last
I am let loose
Into all that's left
Unseen
No longer bound
to the mouths
Devouring me
silent screams

I'll go play with the stars!
Dancing spirit,
Above locked cars!
Shrouding fog-
The city's smog!
High above the rises and crowds,
Shimming proud!
Guide my hands!
Breaking apart
My locks.
For all I was,
Will be lost.
Burning comets,
Crashing.
Raging within,
And without
Passion.

The memories of summer

The memories of summer
Beneath the violet sunset
we rest
The warmth of today
Walking under sleeping skies
While the sun
quietly crept away
Sweat and laughter
The times we chased after
And the relief of sitting beneath
an old Oak's shade
The residue left
Was everything
But isn't permanent
What is really?
Tell me on that darkened porch
What music did we hear?
What songs id keep so near?
When I was but a lonely remnant
What's still left of me that's sincere?
Tell me my name
Who I was?
What might I say to you?
That might chase away
The cold creeping in each day
Couldn't you just sit
Here on this single step porch
and stay?
Tell me there's something warm left

From the memory
Of our sunny daze

All things change
The green grass
Buried in the snow
Brown leaves upon the vines
In time they will change
Bloom a new glow in-
Time
I wish
I ad time
To tell you all the things
I wanted to say
For all I have
All you gave
It seems like the one thing
That slips away
In time
You'll change
Go along another road
I'll remain
Sleeping slaves to age
So fast
And how slow
A moment in the breeze
My mind slipping away
Late nights of broken grace
Like plates
Eyes are closing
My last words to you
My runaway
Where did you go?

I'll run away from truths
Melting into the background
Gripping the words-
Ah
They're gone!
Carried away by the wind
I'm left starring
At the passing cars
Clouds mocking
In their lethargic repertoire
I'm laughing at silence
Wondering just how far,
I've been traveling
Just to become lost
After all those wasted nights
Staring at these mocking
Fucking cards

It's all said and done
The journeys over, your time has come
Rest with me, At the fireside
Tell me, What's Left behind?
What's only begun?
The questions left unasked,
How far did you try and run?
Beneath the city's lights?
Or along the western shore?
Coming home was weary
So oft' you find your heart
Full of storms
And your thoughts
Grey yet spoken
The sky is clear now
The water is cool
The fireside warm
You fought your hardest
Never asking for more
Rest now my friend
You've played your hand
Settled all these sorry scores
Take a breath
Sleep well
On the beds
Two lips,
We are is a breath
Nothing much less
Who needs anymore?

The bleeding script
Of unspoken words
Here on
the canvas blank
Are only
churning sands
Shifting beneath
the preserved sky
The hourglass
in which we all stand
Rising like tides
In the silence
I'll reside
Watching the hands creeping
As their mouths close
Taken under
the burning grains
That so often hide,
Trapped in this nameless,
Disguise
So much more I'd want
To seize
But what strengths in you
Might I confide
To make sense of the silent words
Fallen out from bleeding scripts
These malformed minds
Here before
the unyielding storm
It rarely matters to speak,
Kind words between us,

Anymore
Still my voice
begins to rise against
Empty stares stuck
in the reflection's glare
Our elusive desires
loud and bare
As milky skin
Hidden scars carved
Over screaming hearts
Falling back
Into our bleeding scripts
And once more
Into shifting sands
We drift

I've lost my way
Wanting to escape
But I go unanswered
Telling myself
I have a voice!
I choose to weather
This courage!
With all the chains weighing
down on me
I'll pull this vessel
Out from the sea
Painting the deck
Black and white
The boards teeming
Of both death and life
Shouting into the sky
Guide and guard my eyes!
Until the crimson rose,
Blooming under tired feet,
Sings to me to!
Rage against these lights!
To sleep against
Their fallen petals
At last
Will my efforts be
To set the iron mooring free
Shouting into the untamed
With these chains!
I will conquer the sea!

Welcome to the shivering mind
Clenched teeth
where breath stinks
Staring into mirrors
Gnawing at fractured images
Broken glass over where I sleep
The haunts of being
incomplete
Shallow pride
Afraid of what I'll see
when I finally fall asleep
Pulsing visions of dismemberment
Playing with loosened teeth
I'm burning up inside
Shadows whisper of symphonic nightmares
Swallowing all of me
Am I alive only in my dreams?
Waking to find
Hollow sockets following
With empty lockets
over dead hearts
Each new link to the chain
A cage surrounding this corporeal disease
I'm trying to break
with searing needs
Only to find
Another set of bars
Binding
Tight as clenched teeth
Welcome to the darkened mind
And by the time you're asleep

You'll have swallowed the same nightshade
To suffocate breathing
Preventing hopeful screams of peace
Blinded by bleeding desire
Outside the cage you'll find
Another door without a lock
Or key

I only remember the past
When drinking away
The impending haze
That tastes the same
But there's only now
How quickly it all
Slips away
I lose sleep
But not on this
You who took what I knew
Laid it bare
While we are caught
Dancing in the sun
With hooks in ours
Looking back
I see no scars
Only images of what was
Not what is
And who are you
But a soul apart
Ready to stake claim
To what's already gone
Let me depart
Make way for the new day
And unforgotten age
Passion displayed
Dawn wailing in this cage
Unafraid
Dance and play
And forget
What you're better off

Throwing away

Music lives in you
And within me
The words of poets long dead
Seeking new breath
Be re-forged
In your furious scribbles
Or are we subject to many gods
Pagans seeking absolution
Of the darkness we face

To be board
Walk across me
Shouting into the sky
Looking steps behind
Find no reasoned,
Reply
Step forward
Without sides
Eyes open
I's hide

Birdsongs

Take a moment for yourself
And step outside
At least open your window
Trust me alright
Listen to the breeze
Running through the trees
Their trunks stand tall
With dancing leaves
Listen to the cars that roll
Past you
And the feet against the pavement
Pitter patter
And how the songbirds sing
In their soothing chatter
Or the trains rolling distantly
Hear their clatter?
Come and sit beside me
All is well
I'll tell you of how the world moves
Constant
But still as well
Just as you lay down in bed
And those tearful thoughts
Fill your head
Listen to them as you would birds
And let them fly away
If you find yourself in constant motion
Find your stillness
in the words you've read

And I'll sing you birdsongs
Leaning beside your bed

Made in the USA
Middletown, DE
19 May 2021